Bucks Point Lace Patterns

Reconstruction of old, nineteenth-century cap-tails, worked in black silk. They have been worked in one piece and could be used as a collar or a stole. Size: 107 × 12.5 cm (42 × 5 in). Worked by Mrs Raben of Amsterdam. The pattern for this particular example of Bucks Point lace is not available.

Henk Hardeman

Bucks Point Lace Patterns

50 patterns with tear-out prickings

B. T. Batsford Ltd, London

© Cantecleer bv, de Bilt 1982
First published in English 1985 by
B. T. Batsford Ltd
4 Fitzhardinge Street
London W1H 0AH

ISBN 0 7134 4868 7

Printed in the Netherlands

The idea to publish a book of Bucks Point patterns arose after we had gathered together, over the course of many years, an enormous collection of pictures of Bucks Point lace; lace for which no patterns or information existed. The pictures came from various parts of Europe, including England and Denmark.

Since there was a demand for Bucks Point patterns, we selected a number of the photographs and made new prickings and working diagrams; some of them are pure reconstructions and some of them are based on, or derived from, eighteenth- and nineteenth-century laces. They have not been arranged according to difficulty, but more or less to width, or to characteristics which we thought made them belong to a series.

All laces in this book are shown actual size. The reason why the selvedges are worked on the right-hand side is that, historically, everybody was supposed to be right-handed and for right-handed people it is easier to make the knotted picot on the left-hand side of the work.

The prickings have been printed on stiffened paper and can be taken out of the book for direct use on the pillow.
I would like to thank everybody who helped with selecting and working these laces. We hope this book will bring you much enjoyment and wish you good luck in working the patterns.

Henk Hardeman

Some introductory remarks

The patterns in this book have corresponding diagrams which are printed next to the photographs and which illustrate how to work the lace. The working diagrams consist of a combination of symbols, each of them representing a stitch.

In the following pages you will find a description of the symbols used in the diagrams and, for the sake of clarity, drawings have been added showing the course of the threads. There are two alternative methods of working Bucks Point lace; both are described in the explanation of the symbols below, although no distinction is made between the two in the working diagrams or in the photographs of the finished lace.

Materials

For the laces in this book BOUC cotton 120 has been used and, for the gimps, DMC crochet cotton 70.

Twisting

In the working diagrams there are sometimes extra twists, indicated by one or more dashes across the line representing the pair. Each dash represents one twist. NB: twisting is ALWAYS throwing the right-hand bobbin over the left-hand bobbin (see Figs. 1 and 2).

Bucks Point

Bucks Point can be worked in two ways.

Method 1
This is illustrated by the symbol shown in Fig. 3 and it is worked in the following way: twist the pairs × 3, cross and pin between the pairs at the pinhole. The pairs remain untwisted here, (see Fig. 4).

Method 2
This is illustrated by the symbol shown in Fig. 5 and it is worked in the following way: cross, and twist the pairs × 3, and pin between the pairs at the pinhole. The pairs remain twisted here, (see Fig. 6).

Honeycomb

Again, the honeycomb can be worked in two ways.

Method 1
This is illustrated by the symbol shown in Fig. 7 and it is worked in the following way: twist the pairs × 2, cross, pin between the pairs at the pinhole, again twist × 2 and cross. The pairs remain untwisted (see Fig. 8).

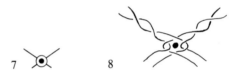

Method 2
This is illustrated by the symbol shown in Fig. 9 and it is worked in the following way: cross, and twist the pairs × 2, put the pin between the pairs at the pinhole, cross again and twist the pairs × 2. Here the pairs remain twisted (see Fig. 10).

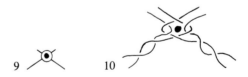

Joining Bucks Point to the footside

For this you will find the symbol shown in Fig. 11. Take care that the pair leaving the whole stitch and re-entering the whole stitch after the Bucks Point stitch is twisted *twice* instead of three times. The pin is put *beside* the stitch (see Fig. 12).

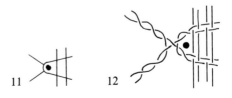

The footside stitch

This is illustrated by the symbol shown in Fig. 13. The worker pair from the whole stitch edge is twisted twice and then makes a whole stitch with the outer pair. Depending on the method, the twists are made before the whole stitch; or both pairs are twisted after the whole stitch in the case of the second method. For the course of the threads, see Fig. 14.

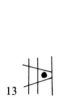 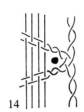

Turning round the pin (winkie pin)

In these laces the worker pair is *always* twisted twice when turning round a pin. In the symbols these twists are not indicated (see Fig. 15), but nevertheless they are made (see Fig. 16).

Picots

These are illustrated by the symbol shown in Fig. 17. The picots used in these samples of Bucks Point lace are knotted, and *not* looped.

Tallies

These are illustrated by the symbol shown in Fig. 18. The pairs should be twisted twice before entering the tally from the work and again they should be twisted twice when entering the work from the tally. To start the tally, cross the pair, the second thread is used as worker and at the end of the tally it is second again (see Fig. 19 for the course of the threads).

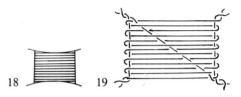

Passing a gimp thread

In all Bucks Point laces gimps are worked, outlining the motifs. In the working diagrams the gimp thread is indicated by a thick line as in Fig. 20.
The gimp thread is always passed in the twist, over the lower and under the upper thread of the pair that is to be passed. In the case of the first method: first twist × 2 and then pass the gimp; in the case of the second method: first pass the gimp and then twist × 2. Fig. 21 shows the positions of the threads in the case of the second method.

Crossing two gimp threads

If during the work two gimps meet and they must be crossed, they are dealt with as a pair of bobbins which is to be twisted. The right-hand bobbin is put over the left-hand bobbin as in Fig. 22.

Crossing four gimp threads

If two gimps come from the right and two from the left, these threads are worked as one thread, the right one over the left one, as in Fig. 23.

Taking out the gimp thread

Sometimes gimps must be taken out of the work; Fig. 24 shows how this is illustrated in the working diagram.
The gimp is passed first from one side and then from the other side in the same twist, after which the other pairs are twisted.
The gimp threads are discarded and cut off close to the work later on (see Fig. 25).

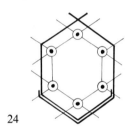

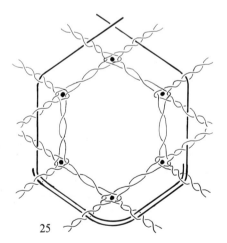

Traversing pairs in honeycomb

It may occur that two or more honeycomb pinholes lie adjacent, so that two pairs must travel to the next pinhole at the same time, as in Fig. 26.
First the stitch is made at the upper pinhole and with the same pairs the next stitch is made at the pinhole below (see Fig. 27).

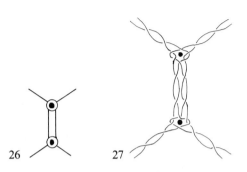

Large honeycomb rings

It may occur that the honeycomb rings are enlarged as is to be seen in Fig. 28. In this case a pair is whole stitched along and behind the pinholes.
NB: the two honeycomb stitches at both sides of the motif are changed slightly; between these stitches and the whole stitches there are *no* twists; this is to prevent thickening of the work. For the course of the threads, refer to Fig. 29.
The left or right side of these honeycomb rings may occur separately in combination with other motifs.

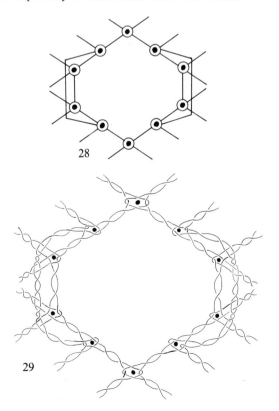

Whole stitches within gimpwork

If a gimp is worked to and from a honeycomb stitch and one or more whole stitches are drawn, as in Fig. 30, do *not* twist between the whole stitches and the gimps. Refer to Fig. 31 for the other twists.

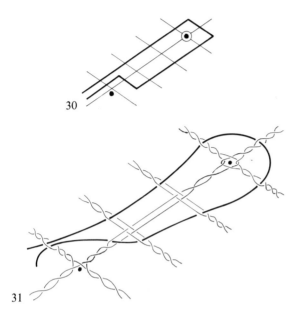

A gimp travelling to and fro between two stitches – with twists

If a gimp travels to and fro between two stitches without being secured by a stitch at the returning point, twist twice between the gimp threads. In the working diagram this is indicated by dashes between the gimps (see Figs. 32 and 33). The motif may also require twists between the gimps.

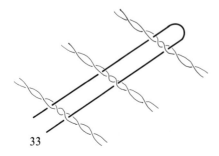

A gimp travelling to and fro between two stitches – without twists

If the motif occurs as in Fig. 34, there are no twists between the gimps as Fig. 35 shows. Figs. 36 and 37 show the working diagram and the course of the threads in horizontal direction.

*In this case twist twice, depending on the method used.

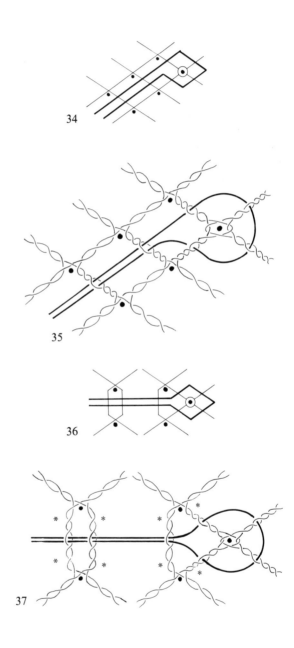

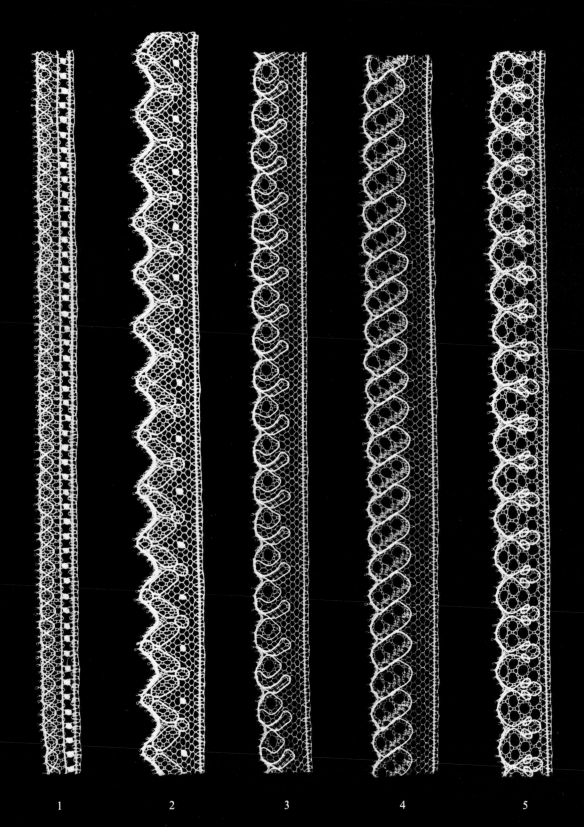

1   2   3   4   5

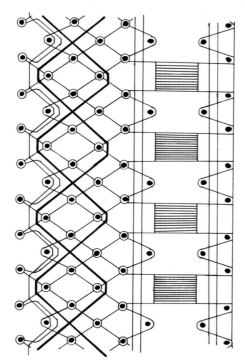

Working diagram 1

Materials:
12 pairs of bobbins and 2 gimps

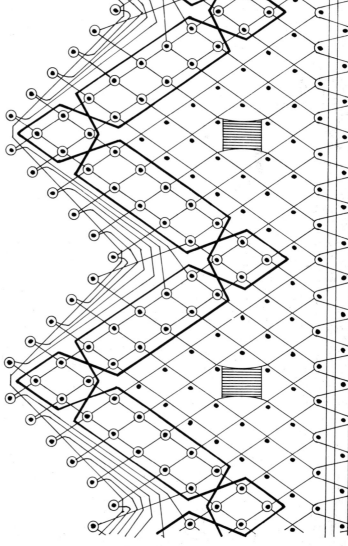

Working diagram 2

Materials:
17 pairs of bobbins and 2 gimps

Patterns 3 and 4

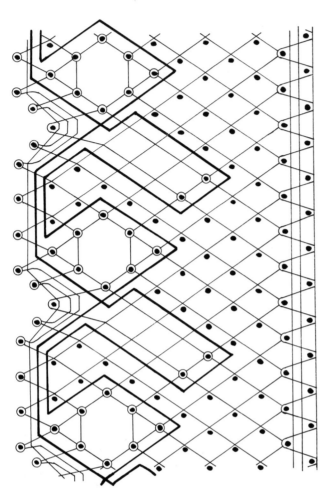

Working diagram 3

Materials:
15 pairs of bobbins and 2 gimps

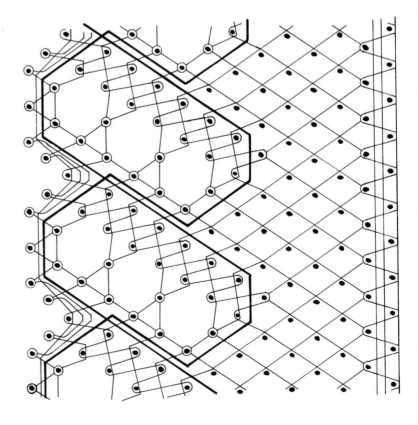

Working diagram 4

Materials:
18 pairs of bobbins and 2 gimps

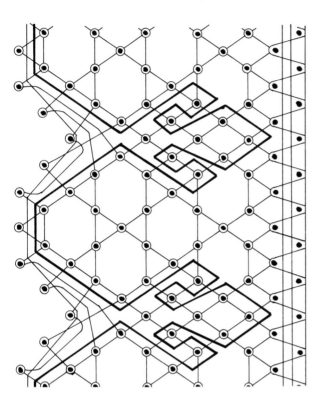

Working diagram 5

Materials:
15 pairs of bobbins and 1 gimp

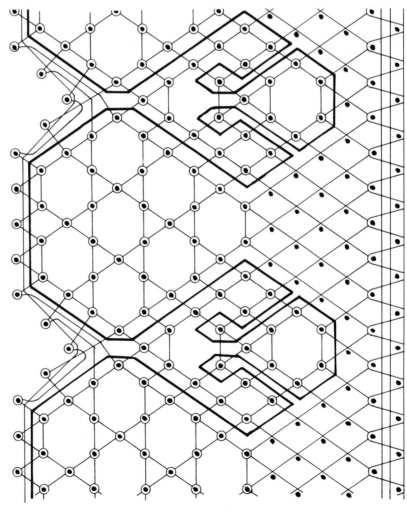

Working diagram 6

Materials:
19 pairs of bobbins and 1 gimp

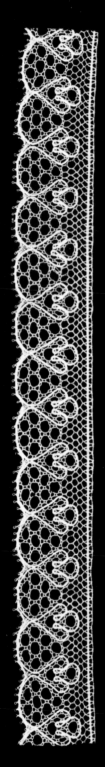
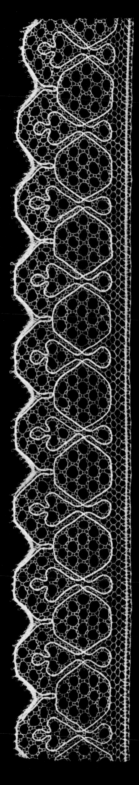
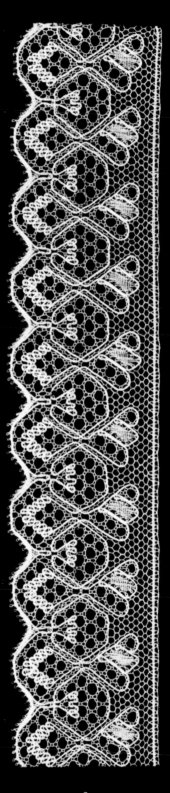

6 7 8

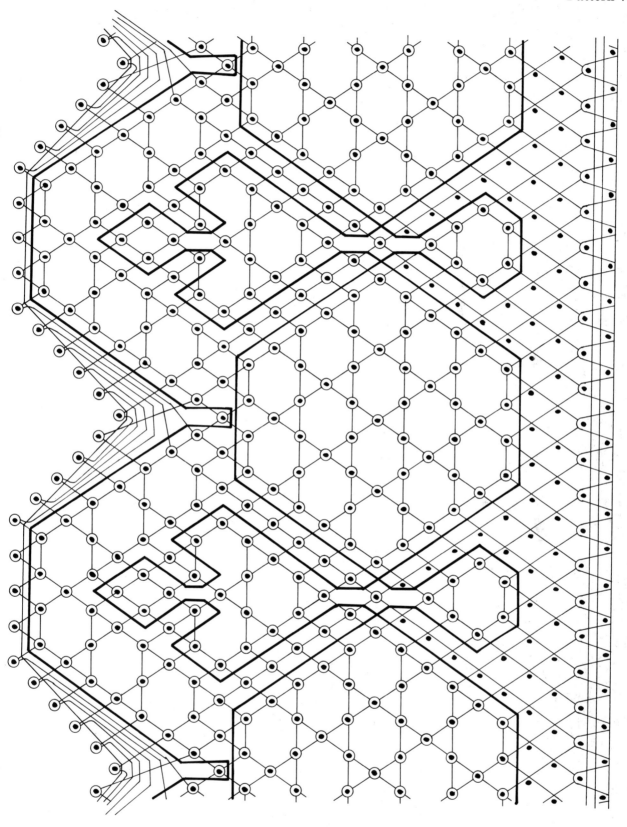

Working diagram 7

Materials:
27 pairs of bobbins and 3 gimps

Pattern 8

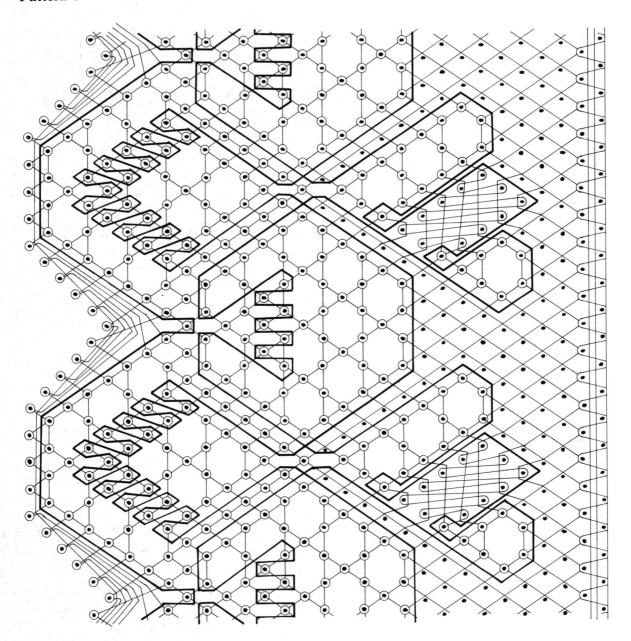

Working diagram 8

Materials:
33 pairs of bobbins and 3 gimps

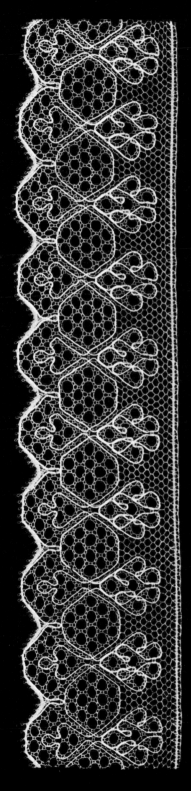

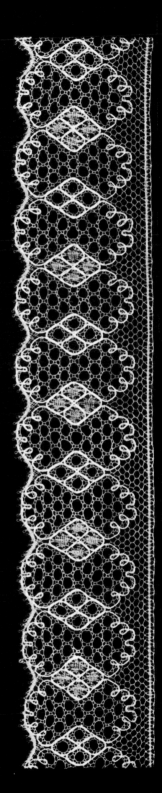

9   10   11

Pattern 9

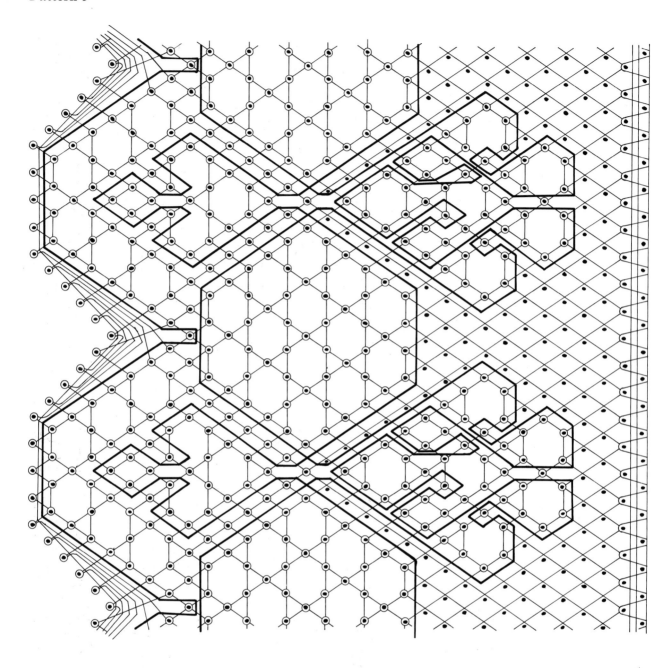

Working diagram 9

Materials:
35 pairs of bobbins and 3 gimps

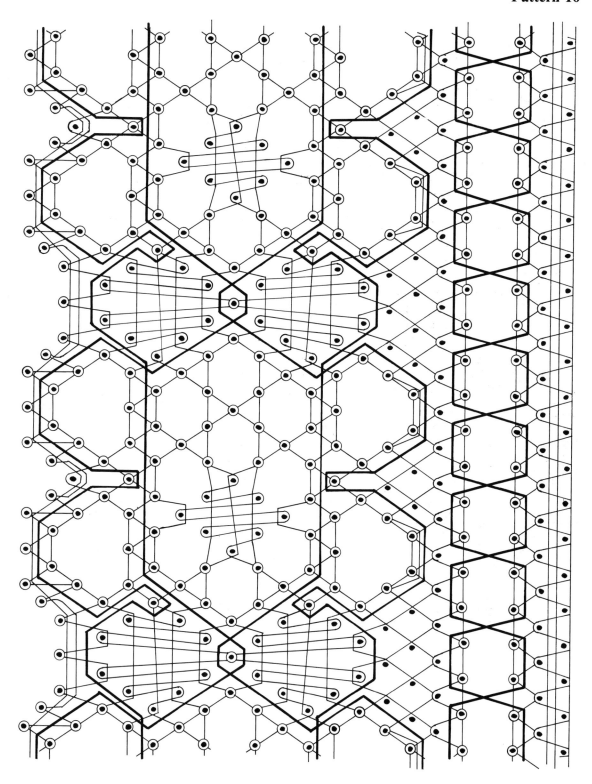

Working diagram 10

Materials:
24 pairs of bobbins and 6 gimps

Pattern 11

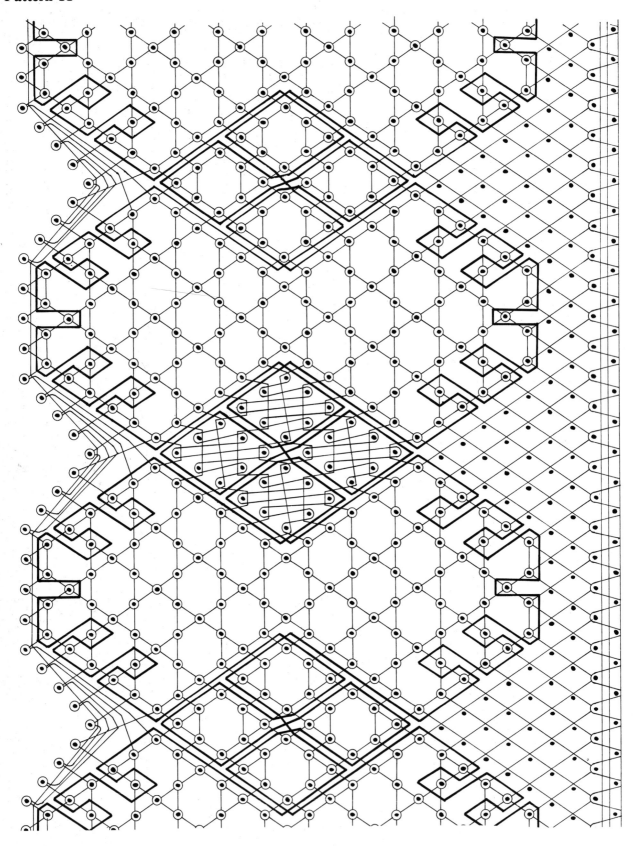

Working diagram 11

Materials:
31 pairs of bobbins and 2 gimps

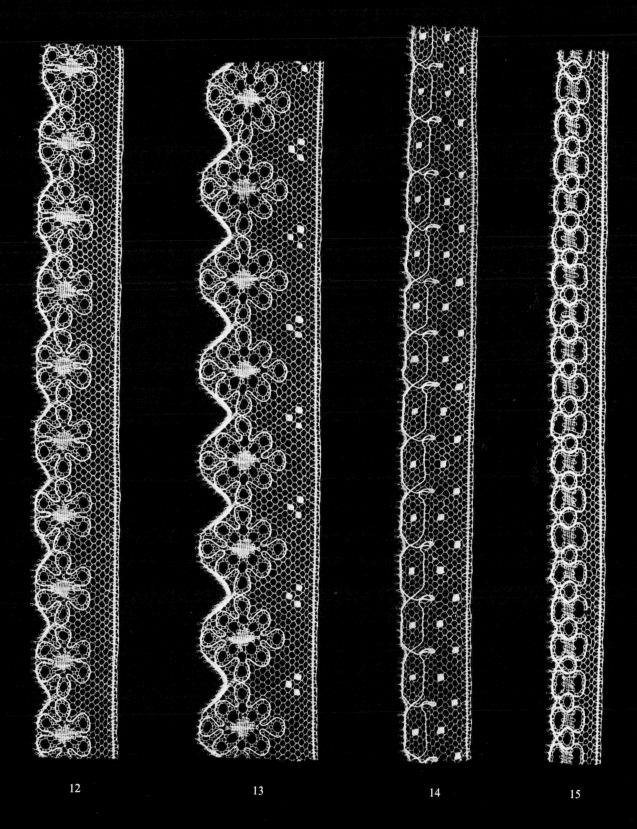

12   13   14   15

Pattern 12

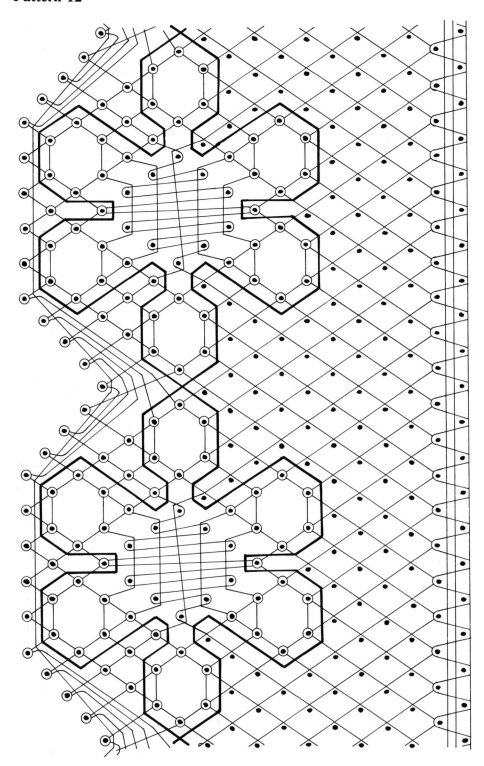

Working diagram 12

Materials:
21 pairs of bobbins and 2 gimps

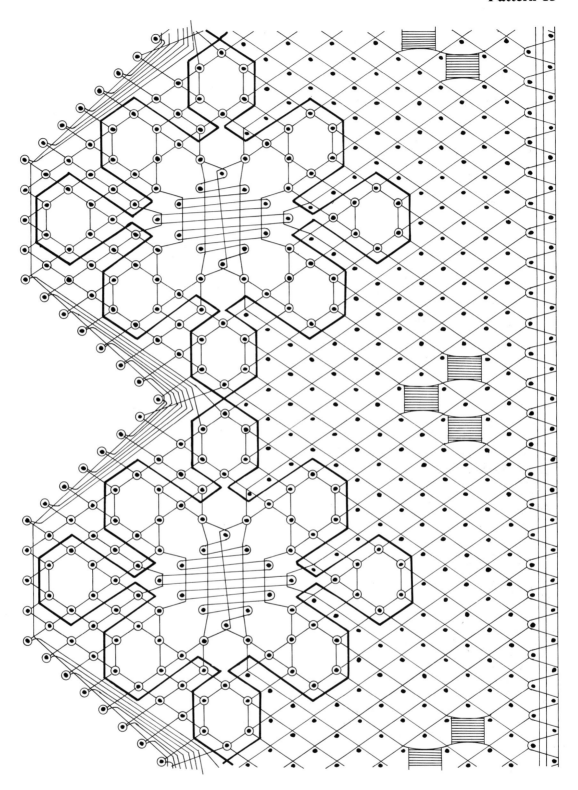

Working diagram 13

Materials:
28 pairs of bobbins and 2 gimps

Pattern 14

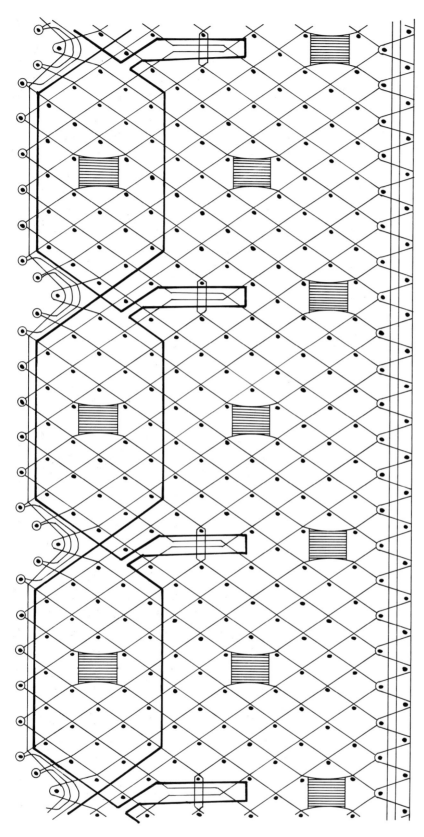

Working diagram 14

Materials:
19 pairs of bobbins and 2 gimps

24

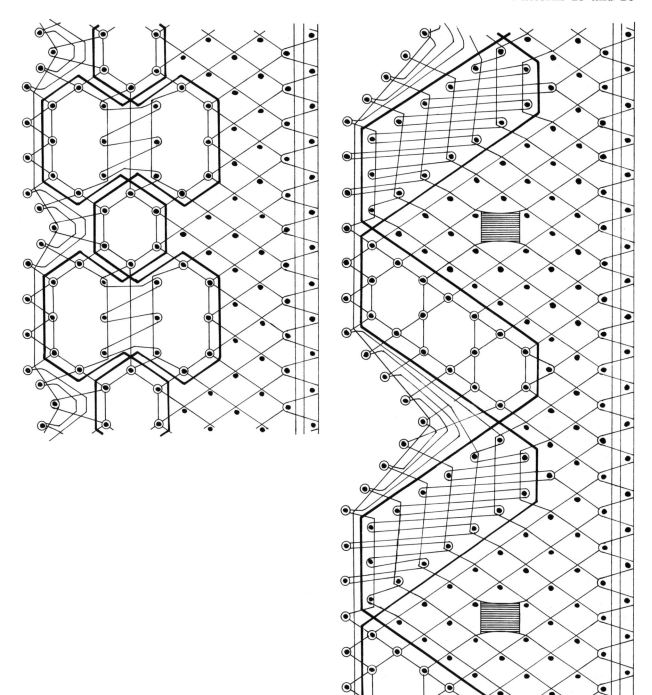

Working diagram 15

Materials:
15 pairs of bobbins and 2 gimps

Working diagram 16

Materials:
14 pairs of bobbins and 2 gimps

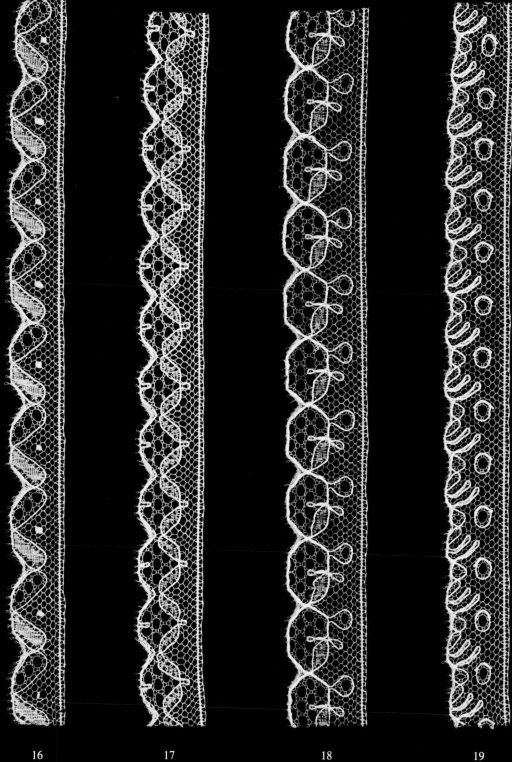

16   17   18   19

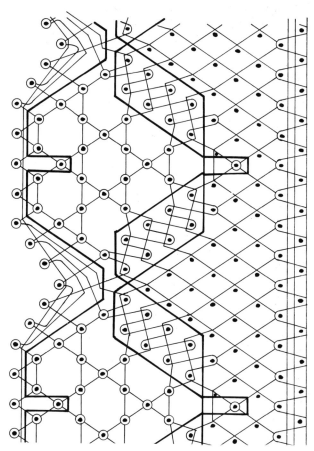

Working diagram 17

Materials:
17 pairs of bobbins and 3 gimps

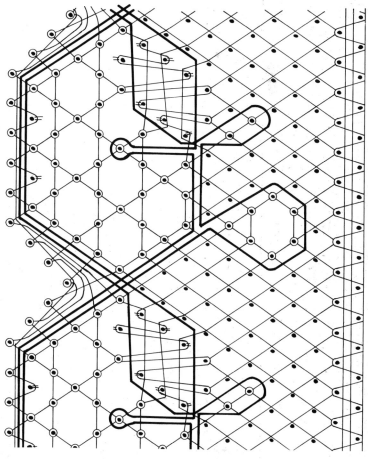

Working diagram 18

Materials:
20 pairs of bobbins and 4 gimps

Patterns 19 and 20

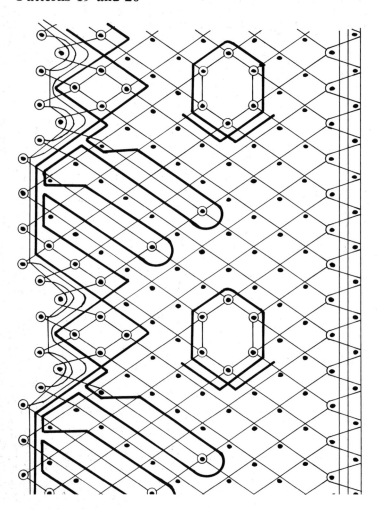

Working diagram 19

Materials:
17 pairs of bobbins and 4 gimps

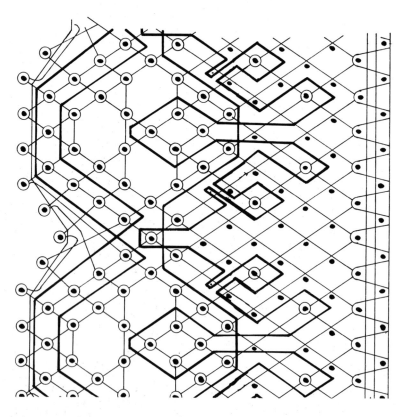

Working diagram 20

Materials:
18 pairs of bobbins and 4 gimps

28

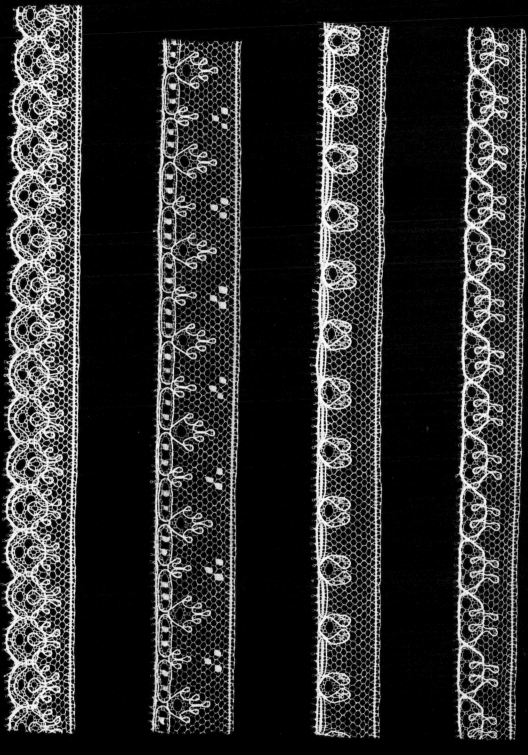

20   21   22   23

Pattern 21

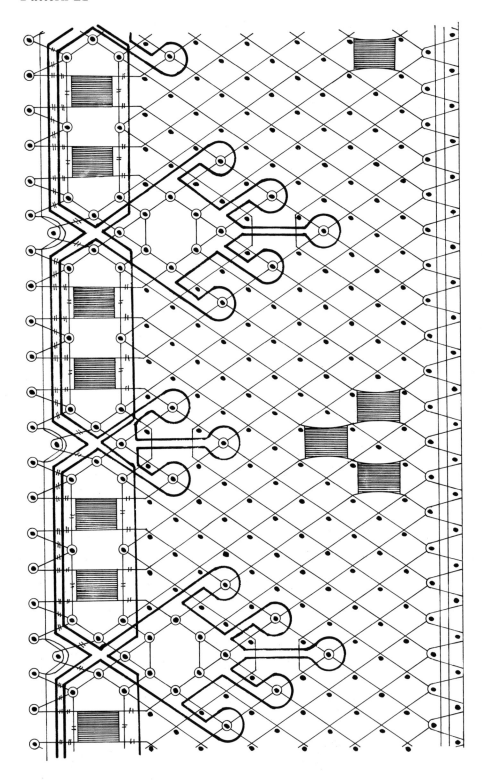

Working diagram 21

Materials:
20 pairs of bobbins and 3 gimps

30

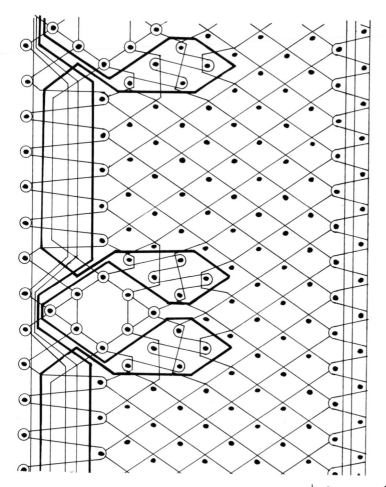

Working diagram 22

Materials:
18 pairs of bobbins and 2 gimps

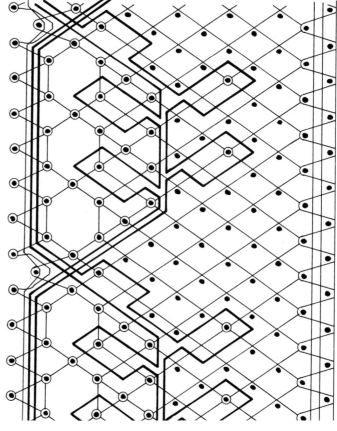

Working diagram 23

Materials:
16 pairs of bobbins and 4 gimps

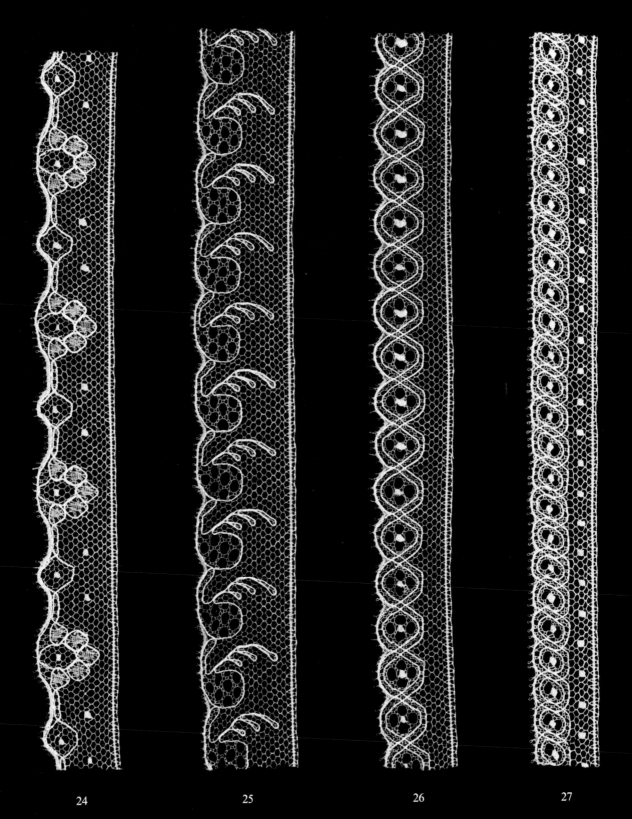

24   25   26   27

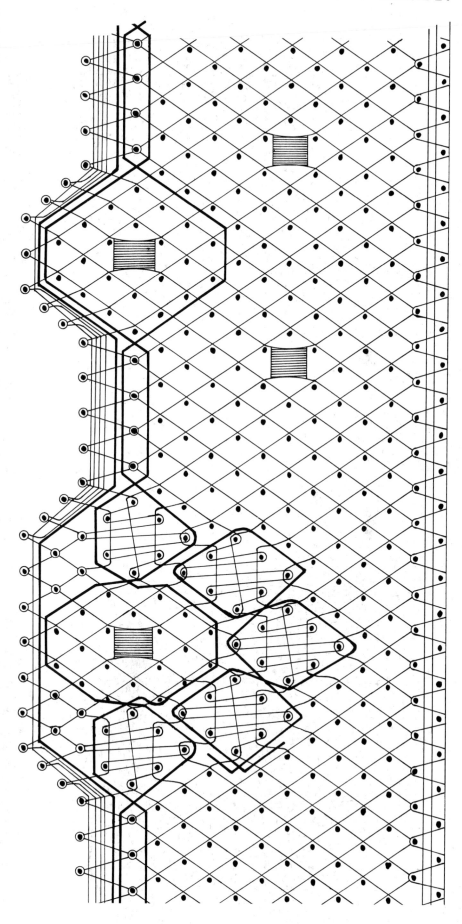

Working diagram 24

Materials:
20 pairs of bobbins and 5 gimps

Pattern 25

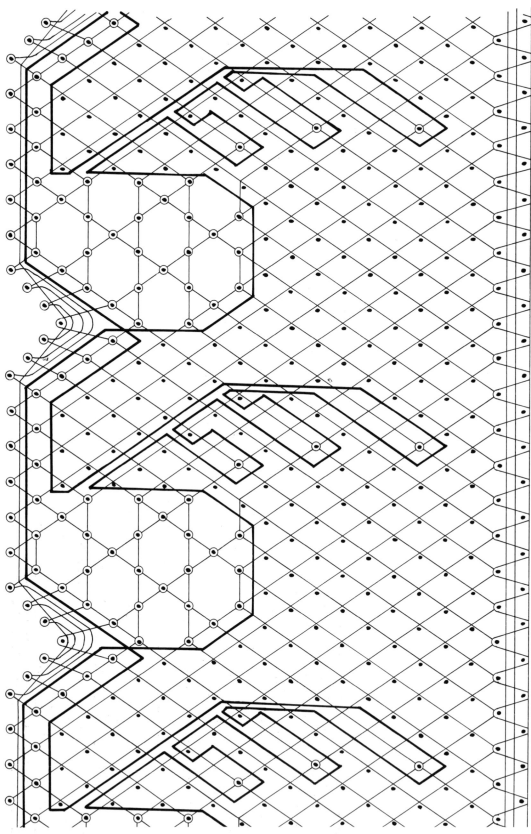

Working diagram 25

Materials:
24 pairs of bobbins and 2 gimps

34

Working diagram 26

Materials:
19 pairs of bobbins and 4 gimps

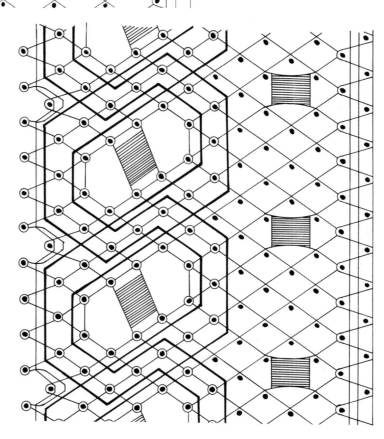

Working diagram 27

Materials:
17 pairs of bobbins and 4 gimps

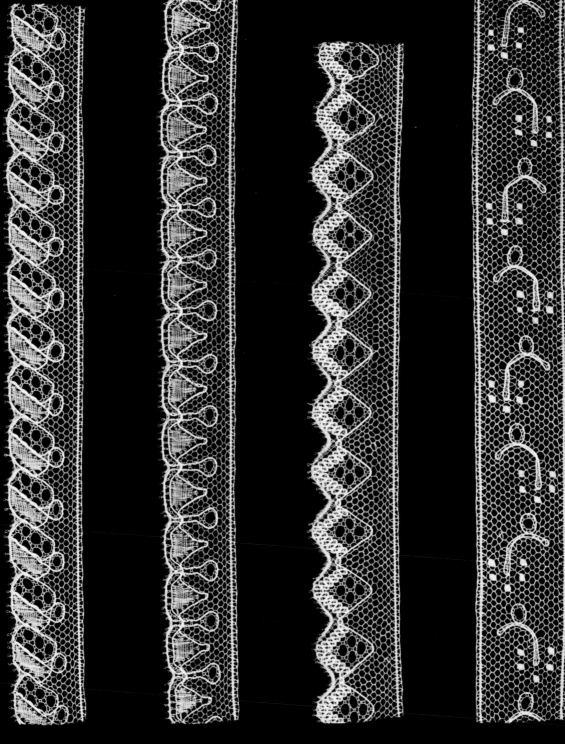

28   29   30   31

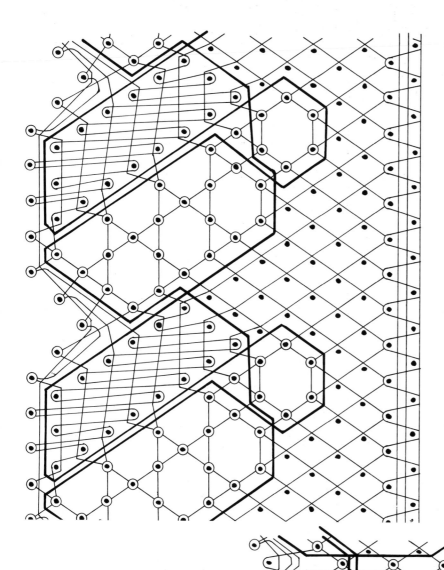

Working diagram 28

Materials:
19 pairs of bobbins and 2 gimps

Working diagram 29

Materials:
19 pairs of bobbins and 3 gimps

Pattern 30

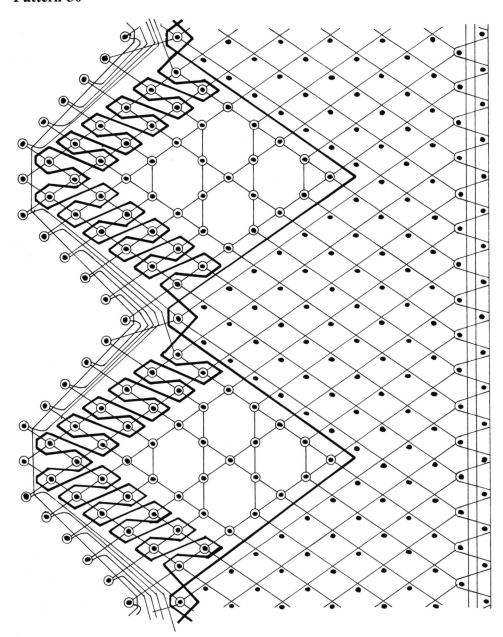

Working diagram 30

Materials:
22 pairs of bobbins and 2 gimps

Working diagram 31

Materials:
24 pairs of bobbins
and 2 gimps

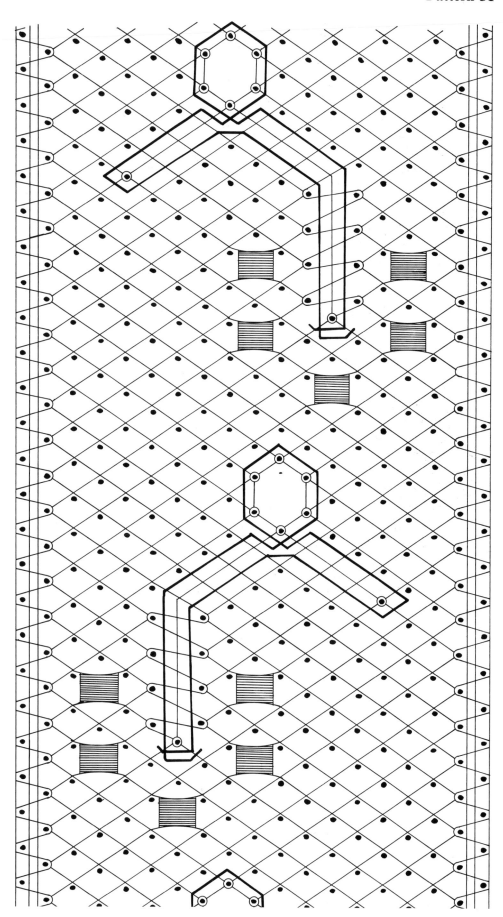

32   33   34   35

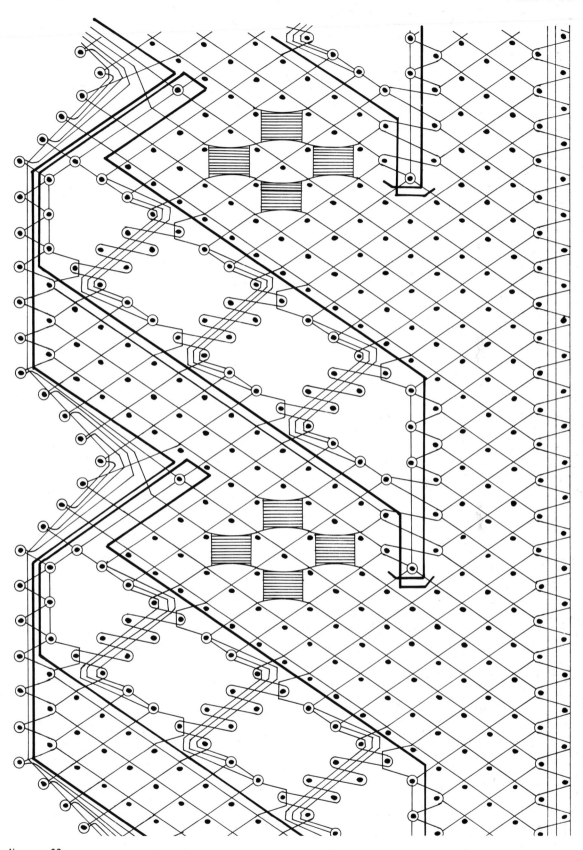

Working diagram 32

Materials:
25 pairs of bobbins and 3 gimps

Pattern 33

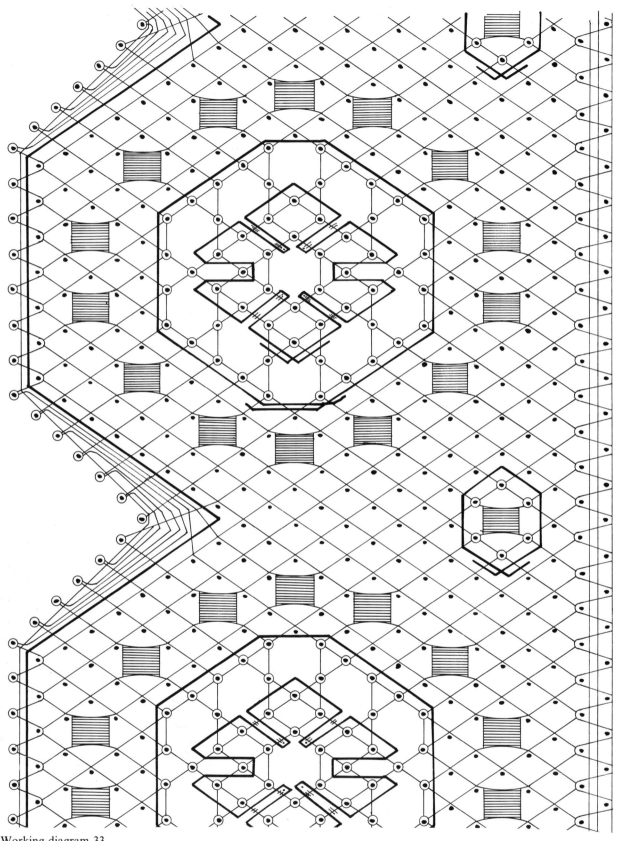

Working diagram 33

Materials:
27 pairs of bobbins and 5 gimps

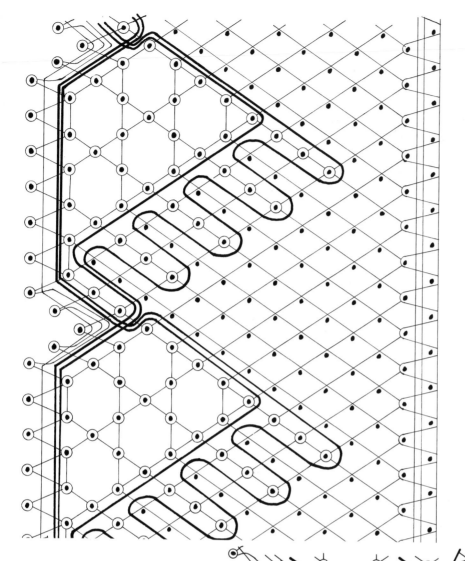

Patterns 34 and 35

Working diagram 34

Materials:
19 pairs of bobbins and 4 gimps

Working diagram 35

Materials:
21 pairs of bobbins and 3 gimps

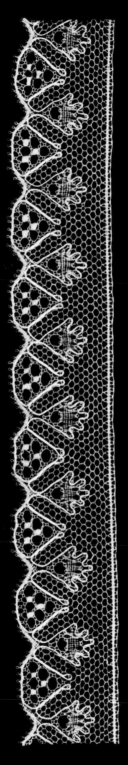

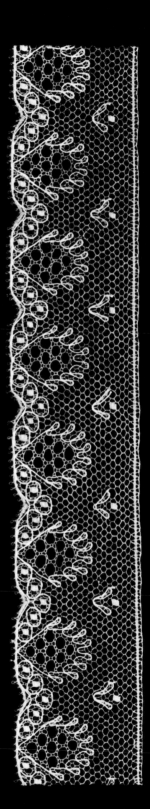

36   37   38

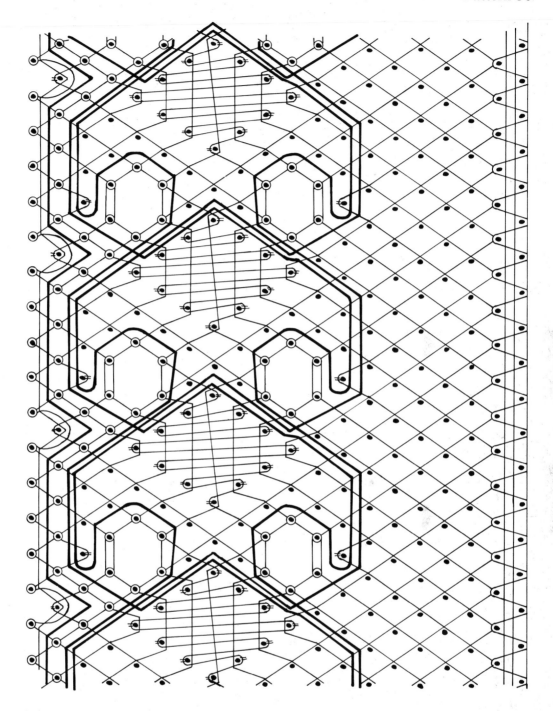

Working diagram 36

Materials:
23 pairs of bobbins and 5 gimps

Pattern 37

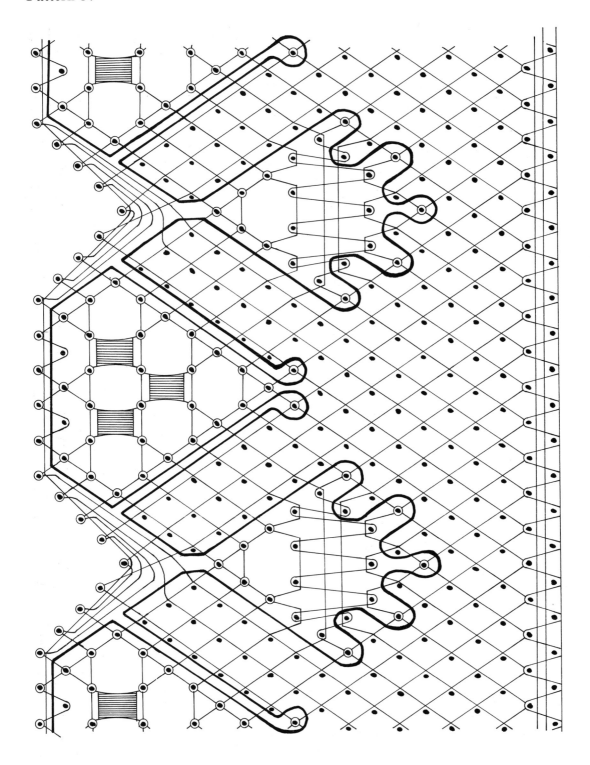

Working diagram 37

Materials:
24 pairs of bobbins and 1 gimp

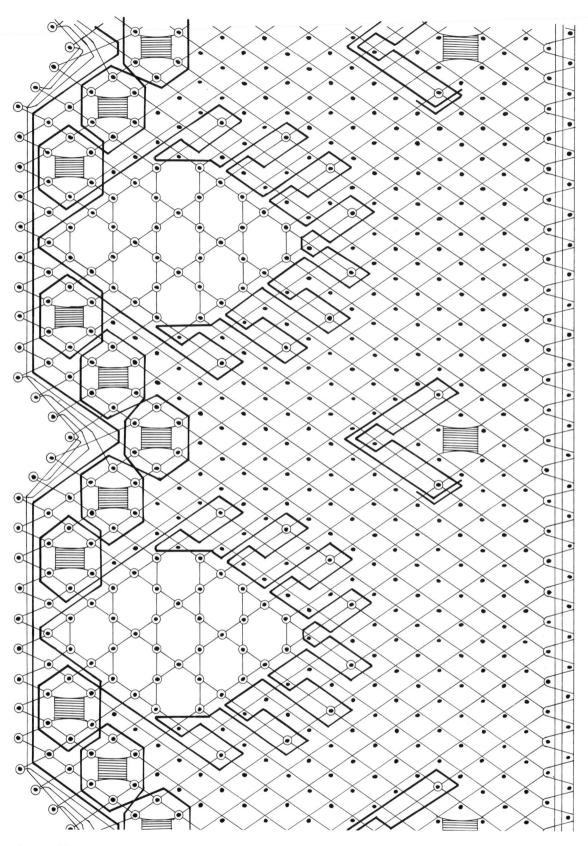

Working diagram 38

Materials:
29 pairs of bobbins and 5 gimps

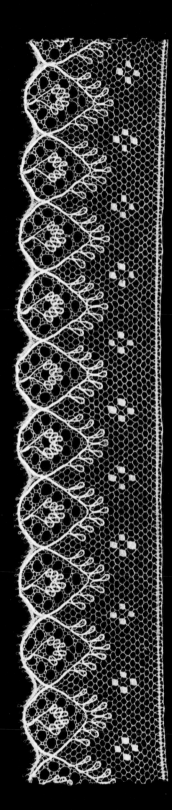

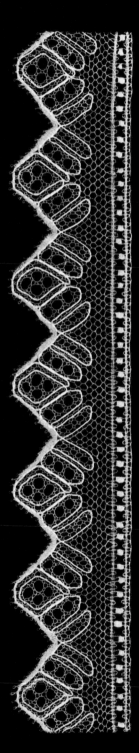

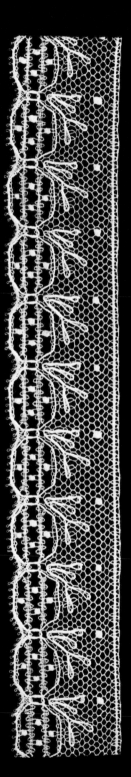

39   40   41

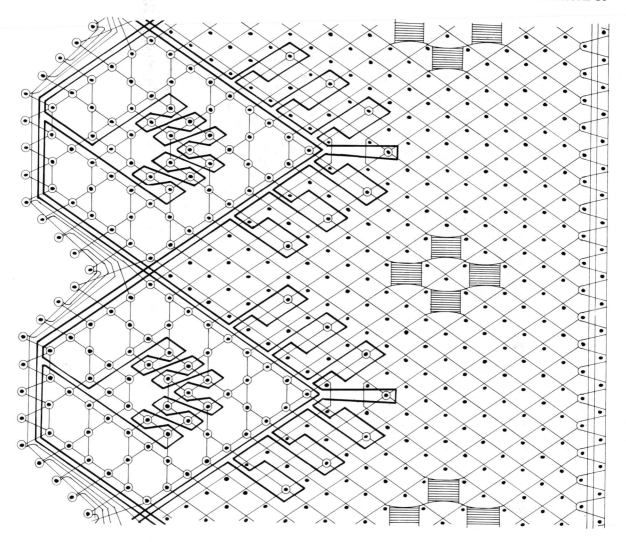

Working diagram 39

Materials:
33 pairs of bobbins and 4 gimps

Pattern 40

Working diagram 40

Materials:
27 pairs of bobbins
and 2 gimps

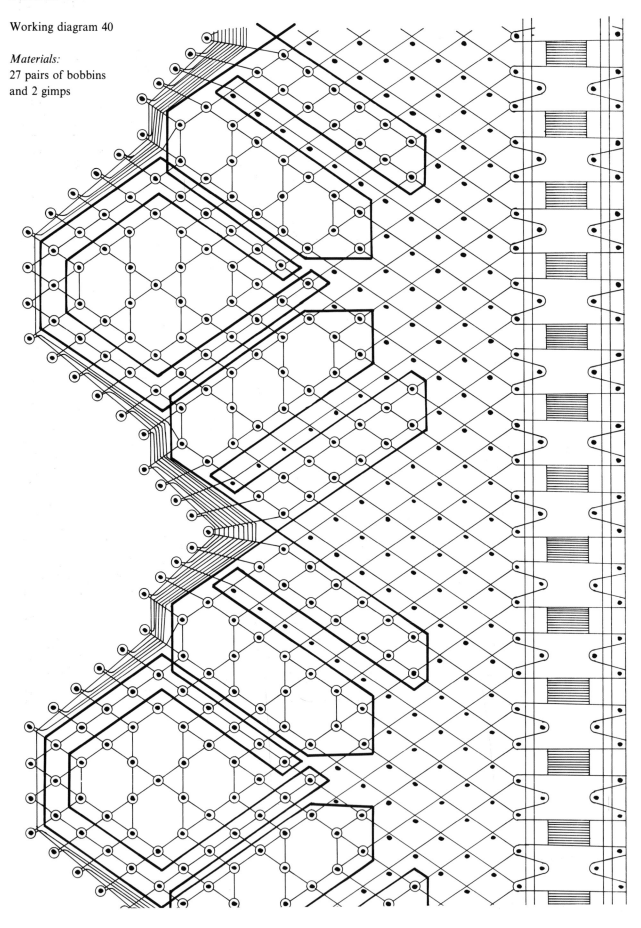

50

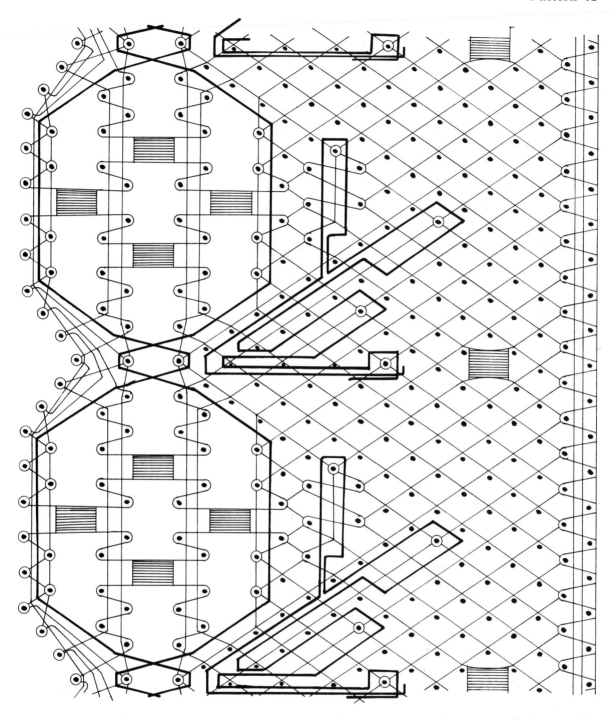

Working diagram 41

Materials:
26 pairs of bobbins and 4 gimps

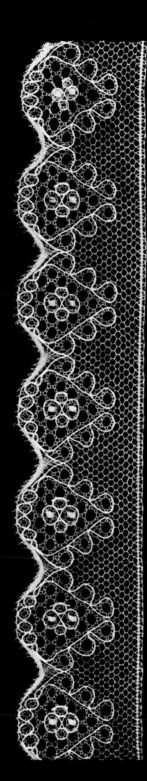

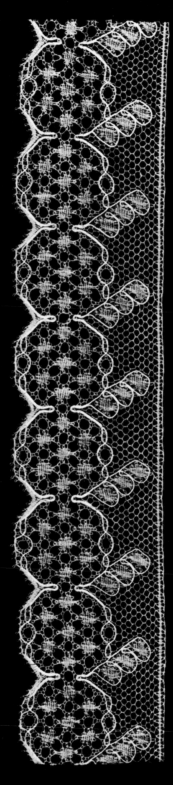

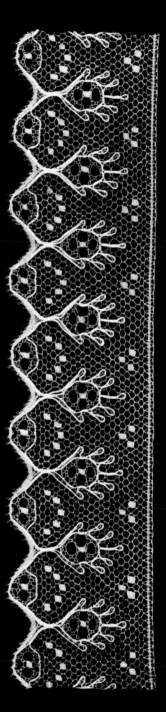

42   43   44

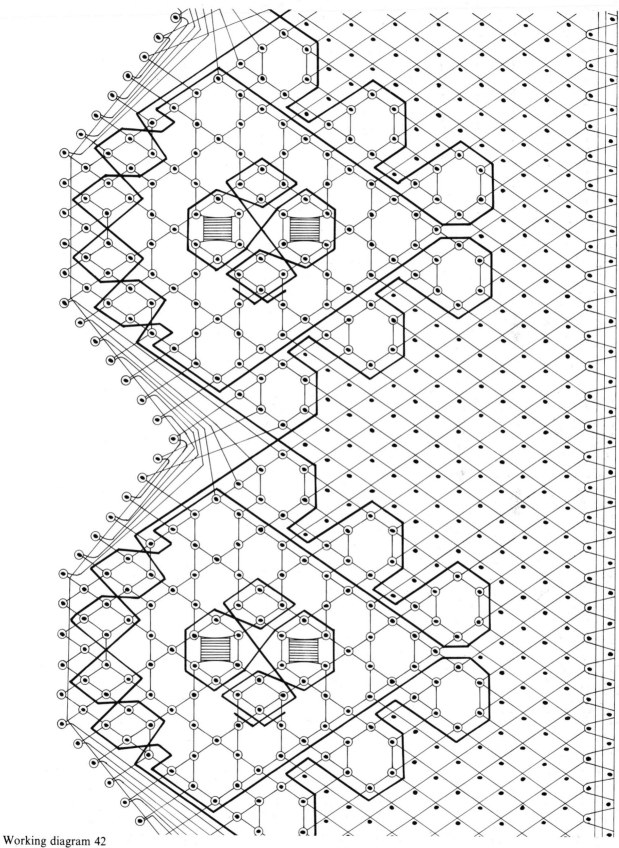

Working diagram 42

Materials:
29 pairs of bobbins and 4 gimps

Pattern 43

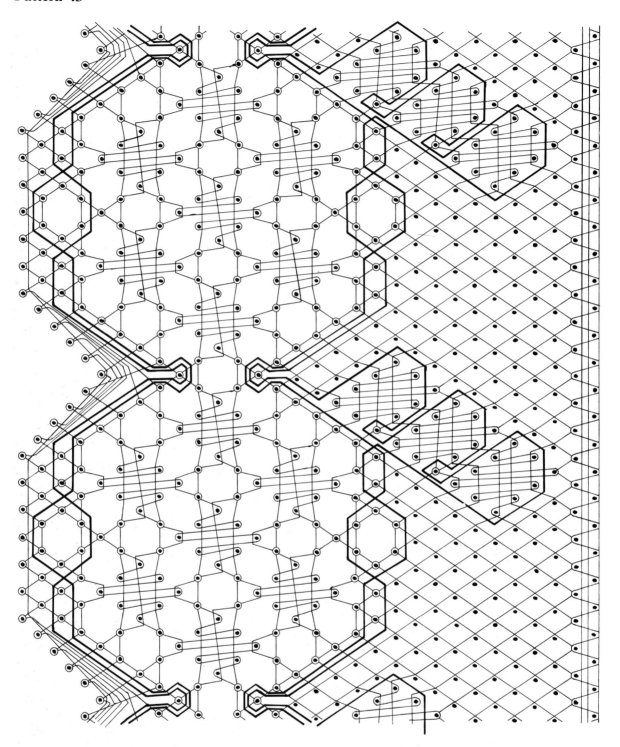

Working diagram 43

Materials:
33 pairs of bobbins and 4 gimps

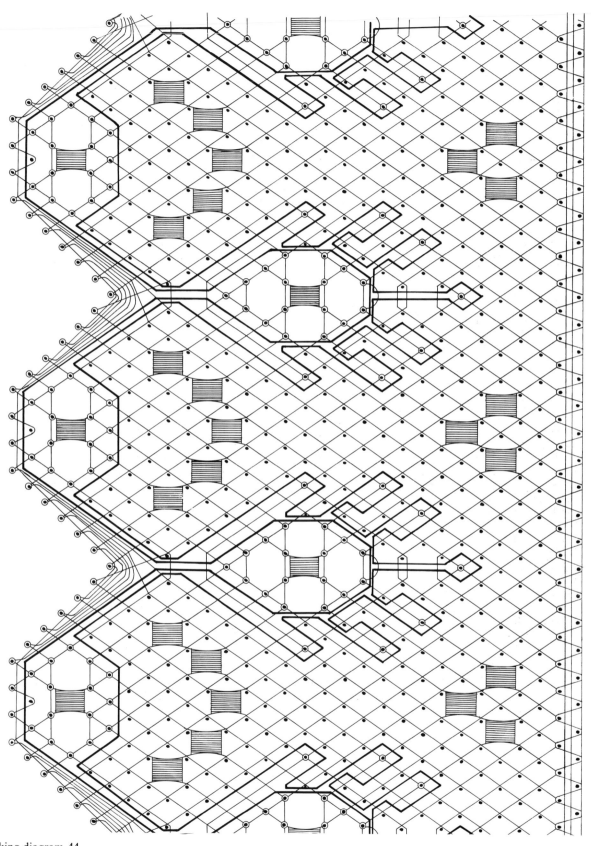

Working diagram 44

Materials:
33 pairs of bobbins and 2 gimps

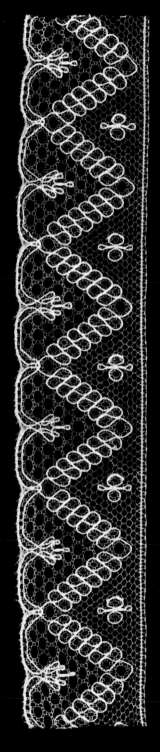

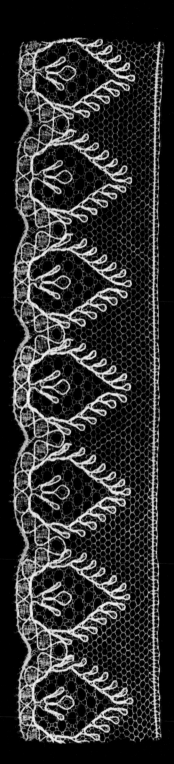

45   46

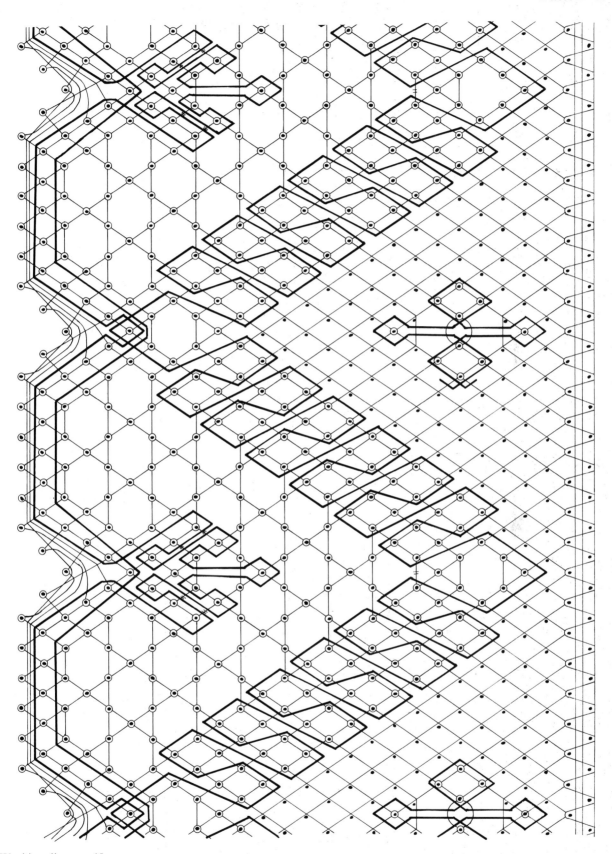

Working diagram 45

Materials:
31 pairs of bobbins and 5 gimps

Pattern 46

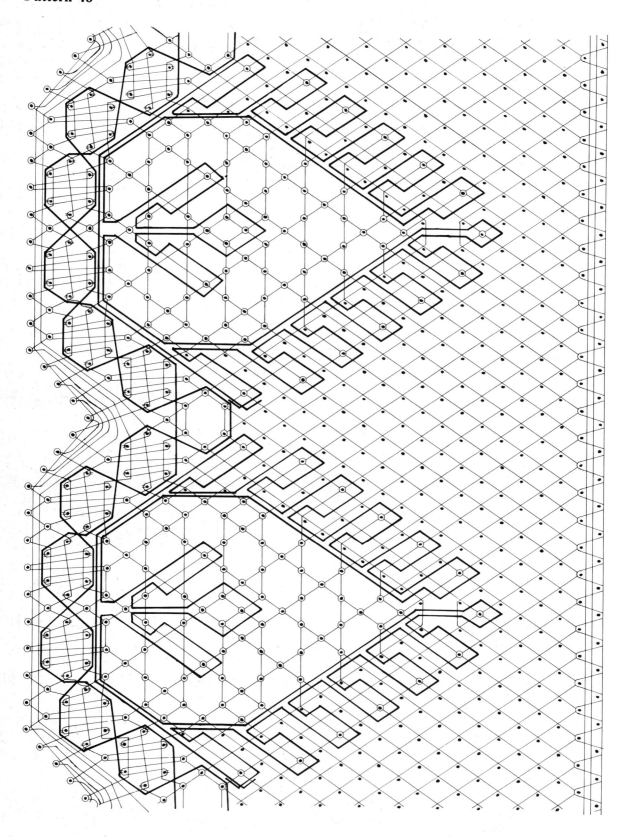

Working diagram 46

Materials:
34 pairs of bobbins and 4 gimps

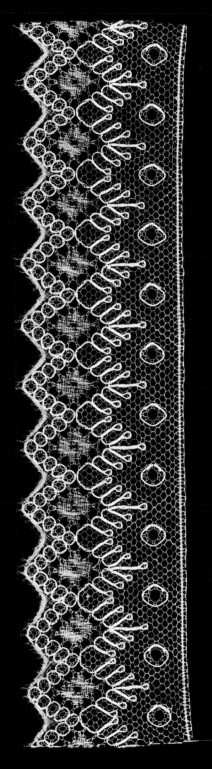

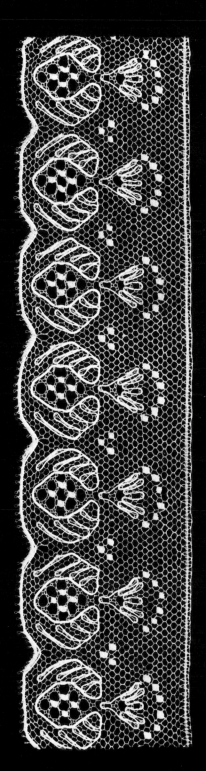

47

48

Pattern 47

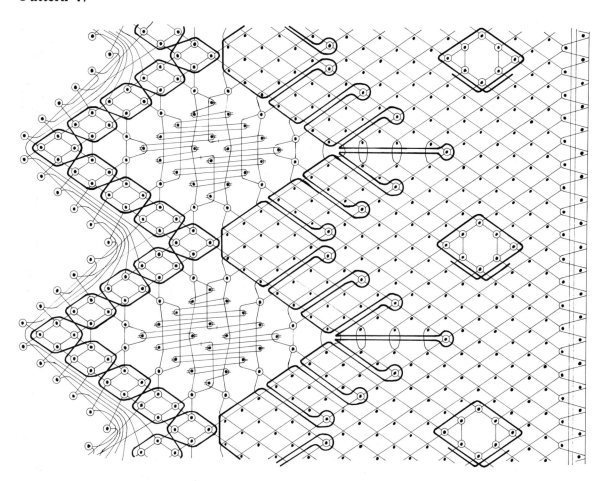

Working diagram 47

Materials:
37 pairs of bobbins and 5 gimps

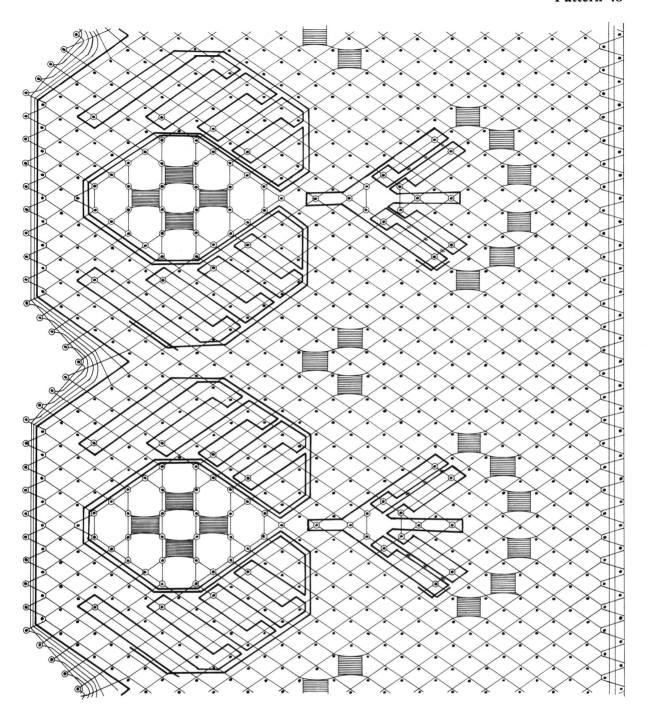

Working diagram 48

Materials:
40 pairs of bobbins and 5 gimps

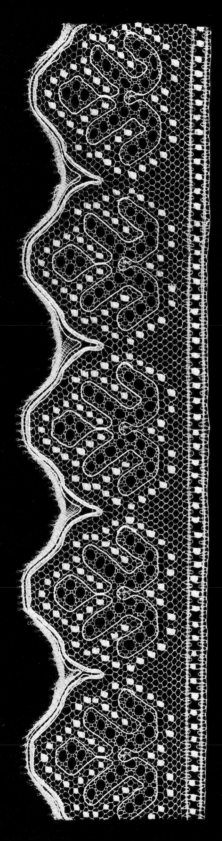

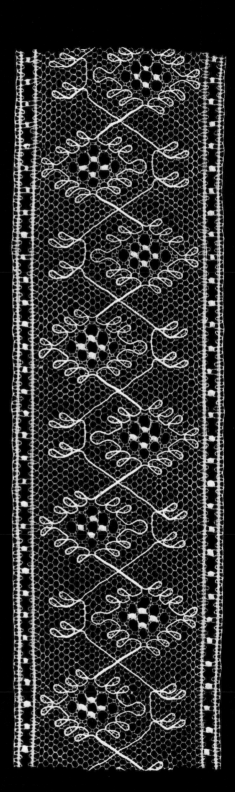

49

50

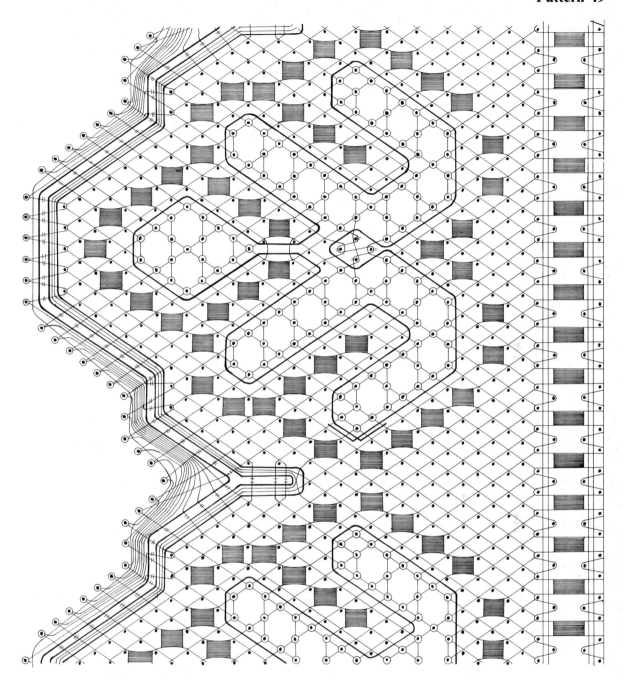

Working diagram 49

Materials:
41 pairs of bobbins and 5 gimps

Pattern 50

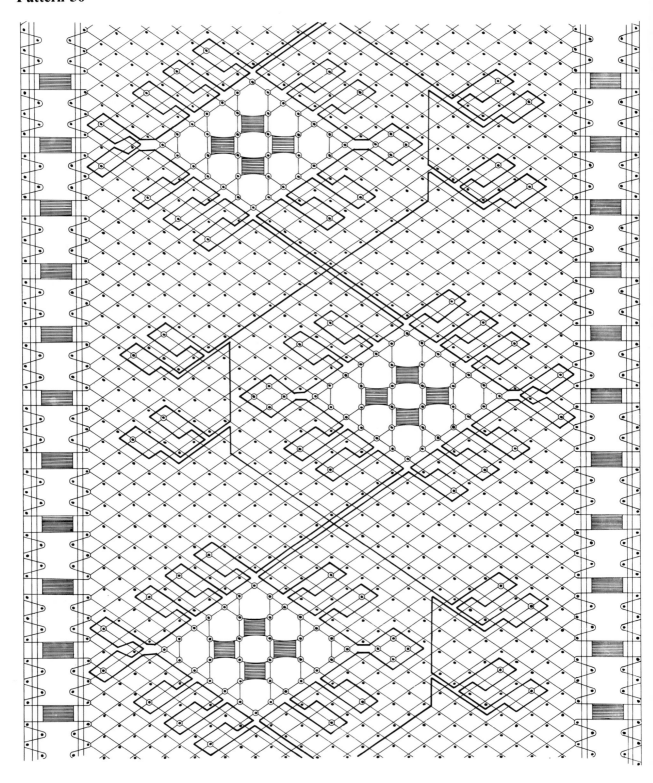

Working diagram 50

Materials:
46 pairs of bobbins and 3 gimps

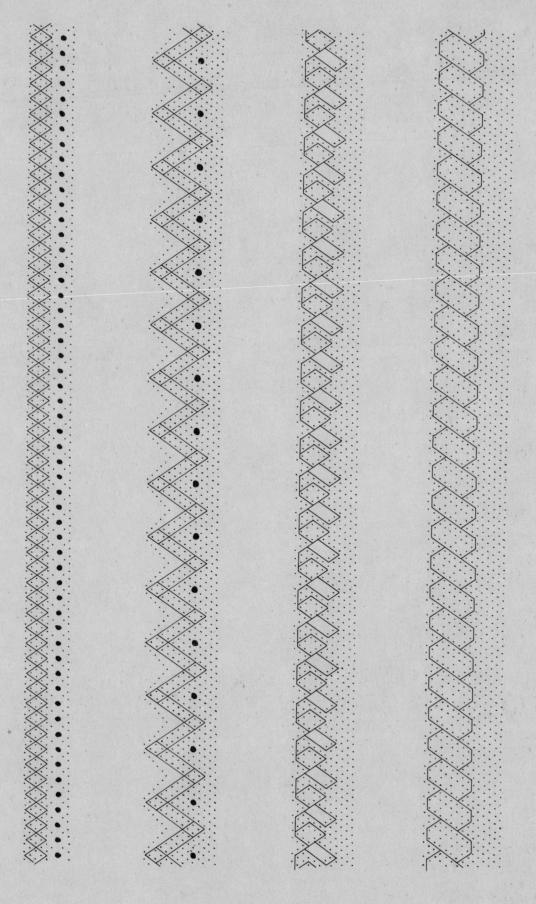

1 2 3 4

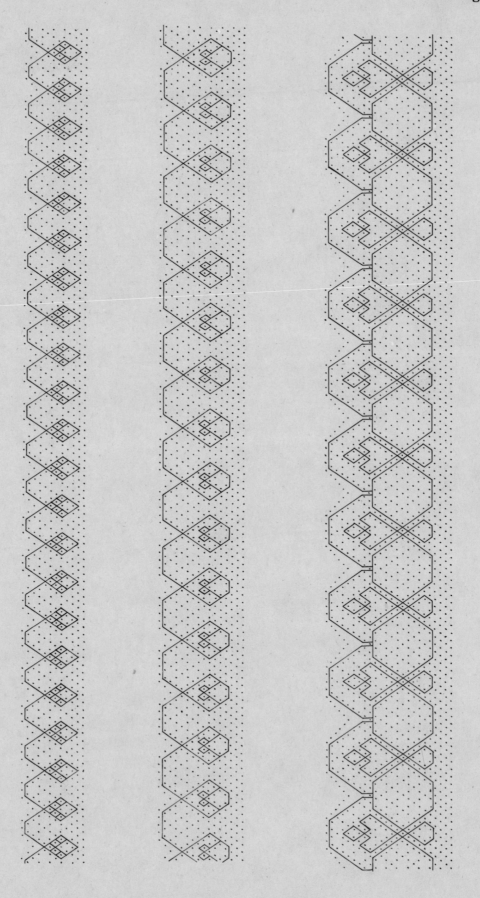

5   6   7

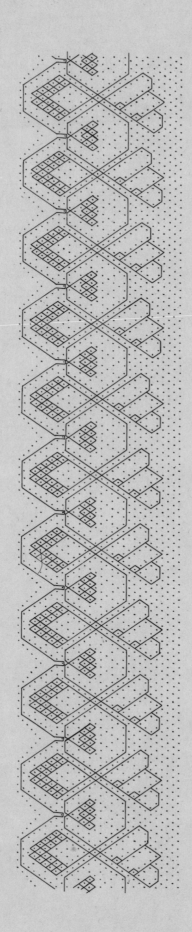

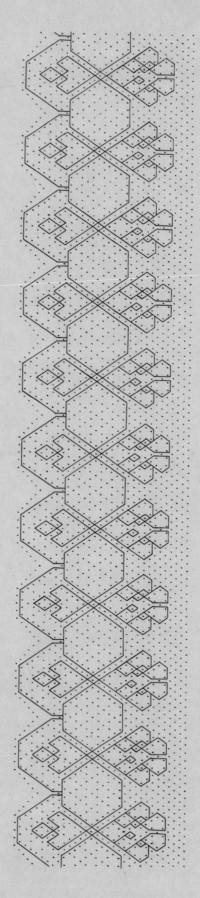

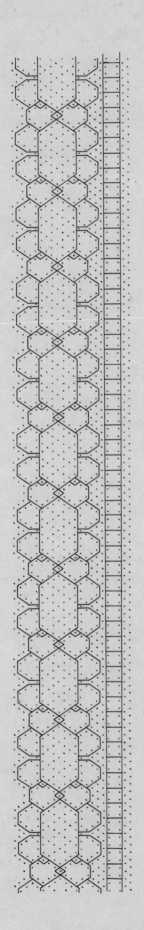

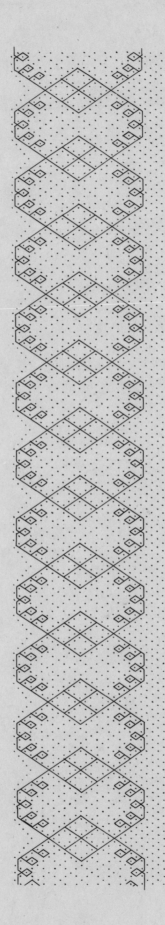

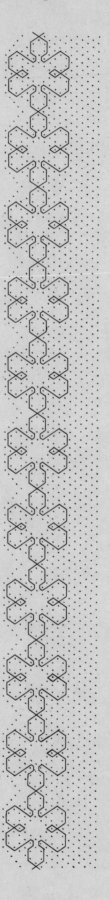

10

11

12

13   14   15   16

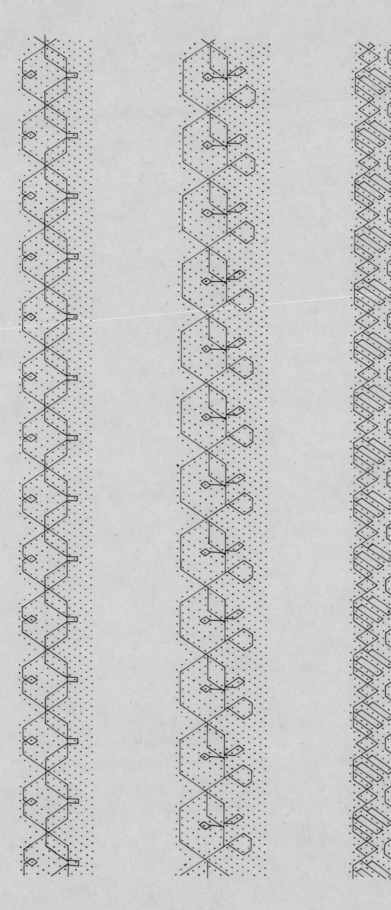

17   18   19

20   21   22   23

24   25   26

27　　　　　　　　28　　　　　　　　29

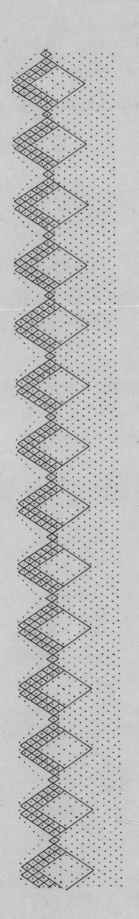

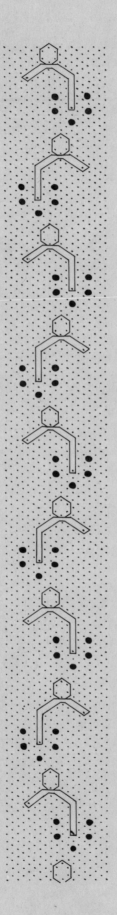

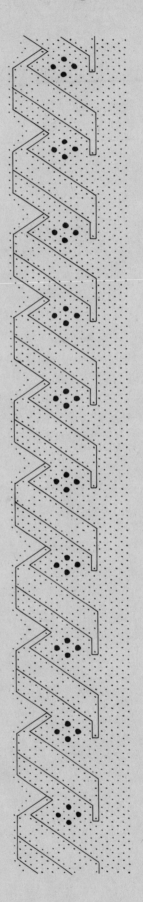

30

31

32

33   34   35

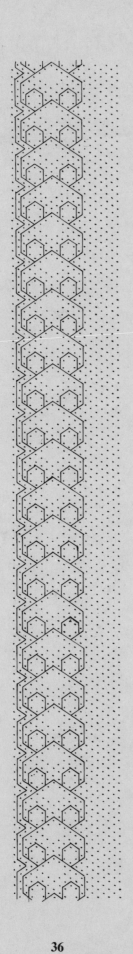

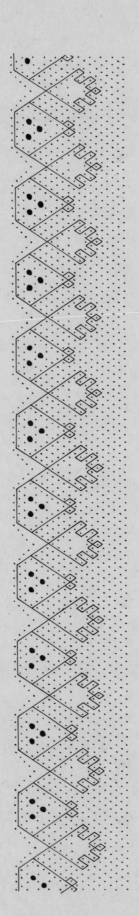

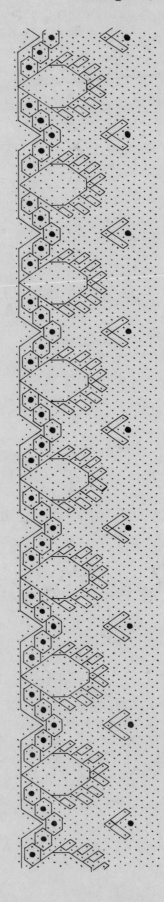

36

37

38

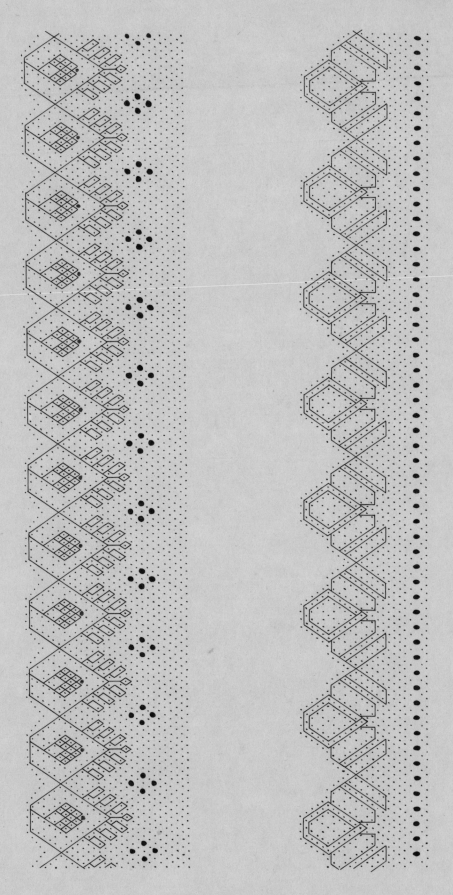

39   40

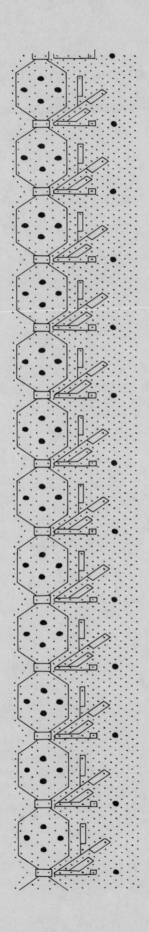

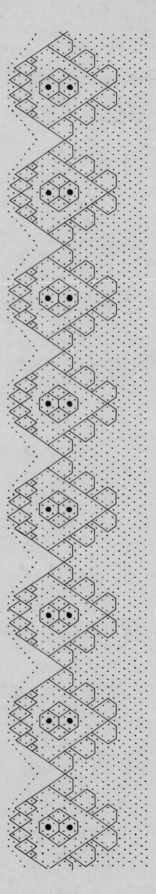

41

42

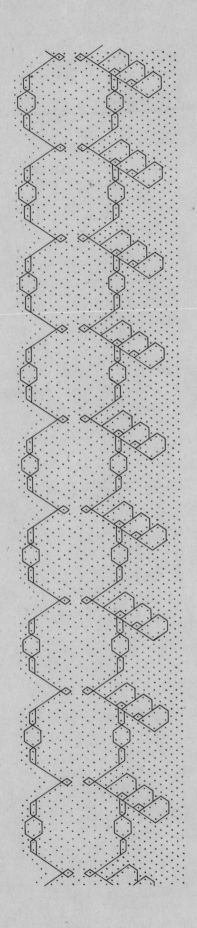

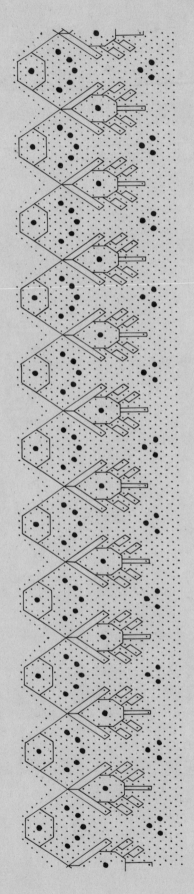

43

44

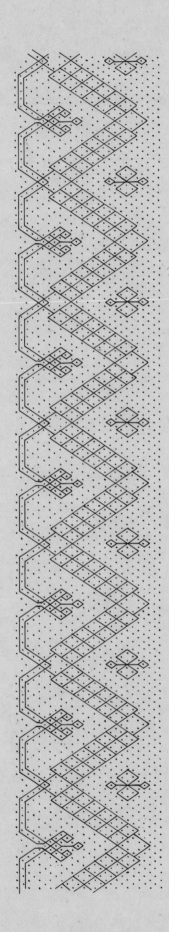

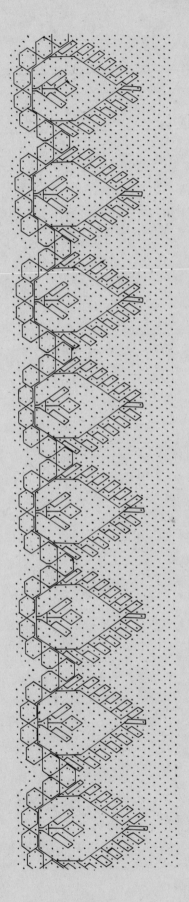

45

46

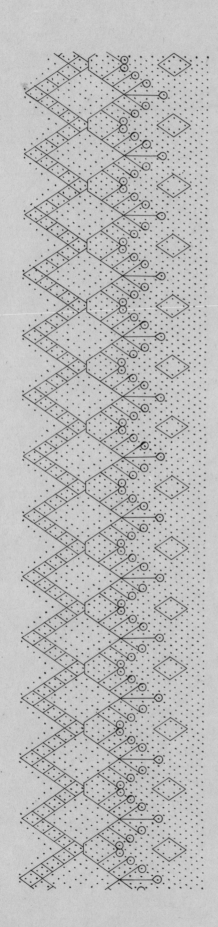

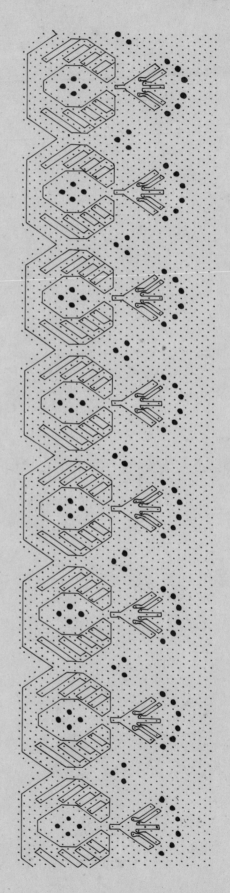

47

48

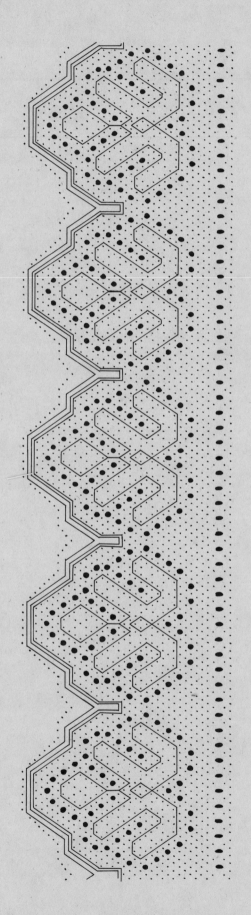

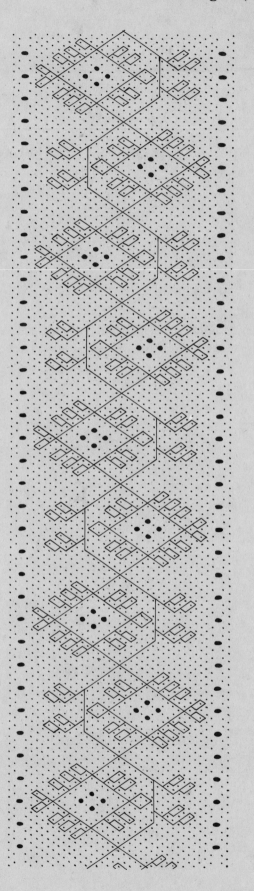

49

50